THE DEVIL IN DISGUISE

**She told him he was smart—and he believed her.
The lie nearly destroyed him.**

A True Story

By

J.A. Marlowe

Legal Disclaimer

This book is a true story presented as a narrative nonfiction account. It reflects the author's firsthand observations, documented experiences, and personal perspective formed over time. While every effort has been made to present events truthfully and responsibly, some details are conveyed through the author's direct experience and interpretation.

Names, locations, and identifying details have been changed or altered in places to protect privacy and ensure personal safety. Any resemblance to actual person, living or deceased, is coincidental and not intended to constitute factual allegations against any individual.

The content of this book represents the author's emotional and experiential truth and should not be interpreted as legal, medical, psychological, or professional advice. Readers are encouraged to seek qualified professional support for their own circumstances.

The author and publisher expressly disclaim any liability for actions taken by readers based on the material contained in this book.

Table of Contents

"Behind every closed door lies a story that's never spoken aloud—a history hidden by habit, secrecy, and denial. This is the truth of Devin's family: a quiet, insidious war waged over decades, concealed by routine and the outward appearance of normalcy. From the moment I stepped into Devin's childhood home, I felt the tension in the air, the residue of old battles and unhealed wounds. The Hall household was not just a home; it was a battleground where affection doubled as control, and kindness often served as a weapon cloaked in softness. What follows in these pages is not mere recollection—it's evidence, testimony, and a warning: not all evil wears horns. Sometimes, it dresses itself in care, in concern, and in the rituals, families perform to keep outsiders blind to the truth."

INTRODUCTION

A true story of psychological control, family betrayal, and the courage to break free.

When Jane Annette met Devin, she thought she had found a gentle, damaged man who only needed guidance and love. What she uncovered instead was a decades-long web of manipulation woven by the people who should have protected him most—his own mother, his half-brother, and the woman who married into their dysfunction.

Behind closed doors, Devin had been raised in silence: praised with empty words, denied basic education, and kept dependent by a mother who understood that keeping him weak kept her powerful. His father lived under similar conditions—controlled, silenced, and slowly erased.

As Jane Annette entered their world, she became the target of jealousy, lies, and calculated sabotage. Her very presence threatened everything:

their inheritance plans, their control over Devin, and the narrative they'd meticulously crafted for decades.

What began as a relationship soon turned into a battle for truth—a fight for Devin's dignity, for a man who hadn't yet realized how deeply he had been broken.

CHAPTER ONE

First Impressions

Let me begin with my first encounter with Devin and the world he came from. On the surface, the Hall family looked like any other unassuming Australian household: a quiet suburb, a modest brick home, a family that appeared regular, dependable—almost painfully normal. Beneath that façade, however, lived something far darker, something it would take me years to fully understand.

I first met Devin in February 2016. A mutual friend had invited me over to "hang out," a casual visit that should have been forgettable. Instead, it marked the beginning of everything.

The moment I stepped inside Devin's house, the air shifted. The place felt less like a home and more like a shelter abandoned after a disaster. Thick blankets were taped across doorways where curtains should have been. The kitchen reeked of old grease and mould. Worn clothing lay strewn across every piece of furniture. On untouched surfaces, years of dust rested like fresh snow, disturbed only by the faint tracks of insects.

It was the dwelling of someone who had never been taught how to inhabit the world.

For a long moment, I froze. My instinct was to run—back out the door, into the car, far away from whatever I had just stumbled into. The silence was so complete it felt staged, as though the house itself were holding its breath.

Before I could flee, Devin appeared in the doorway.

He greeted us shyly, shoulders hunched, eyes downturned. My First Impression of Devin was that he seemed awkward inside his own body—painfully thin, his curved spine shaping the way he walked and stood. During dinner, I watched him fumble with his fork, gripping it like a tool he had never been taught to use.

Later, during small talk, Devin mentioned—almost casually—that he couldn't read or write. I laughed reflexively, assuming it was a joke. How could anyone be entirely illiterate in modern Australia, especially someone raised in a working-class family with access to schooling?

But the look in his eyes told me everything.

He wasn't joking.

He was confessing.

Only later would I learn the truth: he had been deliberately kept illiterate by his mother, Salina, who believed ignorance was a form of control.

A year passed before I met his family. By then, Devin and I had begun dating. He took me to the house he grew up in, a modest brick home in another suburb, its curtains perpetually closed, as though sunlight itself were a threat.

James Hall, his father, answered the door. A towering, six-foot-two retired truck driver, his hands bore the scars of long highways and hard years. He greeted us gently, with a distracted kindness that felt practiced rather than joyful. His nights, Devin told me, dissolved quietly into beers and television.

And then there was Salina.

A gambler. A master of appearances. The kind of woman who smiled sweetly while her eyes measured every movement in the room. She was small—barely four feet eleven—with a slight limp that caused her to tilt when she walked. To an outsider, she might have seemed maternal, fragile, even kind. But nothing in her manner ever felt accidental.

James had raised not only Devin but also Salina's older son, Miles Watson. Miles was everything Devin was never allowed to be confident, polished, articulate. He had been raised in Salina's light, while Devin had been left in her shadow. Miles drifted from job to job—painting, odd labor, casual contracts—while Devin worked the same factory floor for three decades as a night-shift machinist. Despite his illiteracy, he earned close to a hundred thousand dollars a year at East Danburg Printing and Press. It was work that required endurance, not literacy. I remember thinking how strange—and merciful—fate could be: that where his family withheld dignity, life had found another way to return it to him.

Salina hated that.

So did her daughter-in-law, Merly.

They had long expected Devin to fail—to drink himself out of employment and out of any future inheritance. My presence only sharpened their desperation.

Sometimes I try to imagine Devin as a child in that house: a small boy dropped onto cold linoleum while his father drove long-haul nights, his mother's jealousy slowly curdling into neglect. His grandparents had once doted on him; he had been the bright center of their attention. Perhaps that alone was enough to provoke Salina's lifelong resentment. She siphoned James's wages to fund Miles's toys, schooling, and ambitions, leaving Devin with scraps. I learned this much later, through quiet conversations Devin shared with me about his late grandparents.

Yet no one—not neighbors, not teachers, not friends—ever sensed Salina's cruelty. To the outside world, she was the picture of devotion: a warm, attentive mother with a spotless home and a gentle smile. Even James saw only a patient, selfless wife. Devin's childhood friends assumed he was pampered, the indulged youngest son.

No one saw what unfolded behind closed doors—how affection could tighten like a leash, how kindness could be wielded as a weapon, how silence could be engineered to smother a child from the inside.

That early cruelty didn't leave bruises.

It left patterns.

Restless drinking.

The haze of marijuana.

The slow surrender of someone taught that he wasn't worth saving.

Devin left school at sixteen, unable to read a single page without shame. That same year, he nearly died in a drunk-driving crash. His leg was shattered.

When he woke in the hospital, the only person there was his father—already a half-broken man—quietly weeping at the bedside.

Even then, Devin believed he had simply failed.

He never realized he had been set up to.

CHAPTER TWO

The Most Important Meal of the Day

The first time I stepped into Devin's house, the air resisted me. It was dense and humid, saturated with years of exhaled smoke and congealed oil. The atmosphere clung to my lungs like a warning. It didn't feel neglected—it felt preserved, embalmed, held in stasis by the absence of anyone who cared enough to keep a home alive.

The windows were covered with makeshift blankets, tobacco-stained and secured with duct tape, sagging like the torn sails of a shipwreck. The thin light that managed to filter through was jaundiced, the color of old paper stained by nicotine.

In the center of the room, an oak table sat buried beneath a sediment of plates, ash, and crumbs. Black rings from coffee mugs had burned permanently into the wood. The cutlery drawer was empty. What replaced it was a mismatched assortment of hand-me-down utensils scattered across the counters—each one a relic of someone else's kitchen.

The sink had become its own ecosystem. Ceramic bowls floated in tepid dishwater, mixed with the residue of forgotten meals. Cigarette butts bobbed among them, as if laziness had solidified into routine. Above the faucet, the tiles were two-toned: pale where grease had yet to reach, dark everywhere else.

At first, I thought this place could belong on a renovation show like Fixer Upper or The Block. But the longer I stood there, the more I realized it belonged on Hoarders or My Strange Addiction.

Dust coated every surface, thick enough to have texture. It collected in the corners of picture frames, clung to the baseboards, and powdered the outlines of furniture. The linoleum floor was cracked, worn, and sticky beneath my flats. It didn't feel like stepping on dried juice; it felt like walking across flypaper. In one spot, the floor nearly took my shoe with it.

While the tackiness slowed me down, Devin moved through the room with practiced humility. He didn't apologize, but his body did—shallow breaths, a bowed head, movements angled inward. Everything about him spoke of a man trained not to impose.

"Make yourself at home," he said softly, smiling in a way that admitted he already knew I couldn't.

"Um… thanks," I answered, trying not to stare.

Something outside the window caught Devin's attention, and he paused to look out. While he was distracted, I studied him more closely.

He was thin, just over five feet eleven, though he carried himself shorter from habit. His shoulders hunched inward, his head angled down, his eyes tilted upward, as if seeking permission to exist. His clothes hung loose—thin cotton washed to near transparency, a shirt with a frayed collar that might once have been white. His skin had that pale, bluish undertone you see in horror films—sickly or vampiric. I hadn't decided which.

When he finally pulled away from whatever had caught his attention, he sat again. It was only then that I noticed the plate he'd been eating from, still balanced among the clutter.

"If you want, I can... make you something too," he offered.

"I'm good, thanks," I said. "I had an early dinner last night and ended up overeating this morning."

"You sure?"

"Yes. I'm probably good for the day. I don't eat much after a big breakfast."

"Oh."

Devin handled his fork not with simple awkwardness, but with guarded caution. He held it too close to the tines, as if afraid it might break. His movements were uncoordinated, his jaw working quickly—mechanically, as though food were merely sustenance, not a source of comfort. There was no rhythm, no pauses for conversation, no sense of pleasure. I had seen eating like this only in hospital wards—patients who understood that food was merely a brief respite.

"Well, you know what they say?" he mumbled through a mouthful.

A jolt of worry ran through me. I hadn't meant to offend him. When someone offers you food in their home, it's considered good manners to accept—even water. But manners were the least of what this house lacked.

"What do they say?" I asked cautiously.

"They say breakfast is the most important meal of the day. If you're gonna pig out on any meal… well, breakfast would be the one."

I let out a small laugh, half nervous, half relieved. "True. I've heard that a lot."

He grinned faintly and went back to eating.

I glanced toward Perry, the mutual friend who had brought me there. Leaning slightly away from Devin, I lowered my voice.

"Why is he like this? Didn't his parents ever teach him?"

Perry scoffed, amused. "Devin's just spoiled. His parents did everything for him."

Spoiled.

The word pricked at me like a thorn. Spoiled things swell, demand, rot outward. Devin was the opposite—subdued, recessive, shaped by an invisible pressure to shrink. His friends mistook his stillness for privilege, his detachment for laziness.

But I recognized something else.

He wasn't spoiled.

He was starved.

Devin looked up, catching me studying him. A half-smile tugged at his lips.

"What?"

"Nothing," I said quickly.

But it wasn't nothing.

It was everything—

the duct-taped blankets,

the smell of nicotine and old fat,

the hesitancy in every gesture,

the way he moved through a room as if apologizing for breathing.

That night, long after I left, the image of the house lingered. The air there had weight. It felt wrong. Perry couldn't see it, but I could. I'd seen it before: in children raised without structure, in adults who learned to survive instead of live.

It wasn't until November 2017, over a year later, that I met his parents for the first time. Everything I had suspected began to make sense.

CHAPTER THREE

Family Values

I remember the first time we went to Devin's parents' house. It was late evening when we pulled up to a modest, unassuming brick bungalow, its lace curtains drawn tightly against the dusk. At first glance, it appeared to be the kind of place where normal life unfolded—family dinners around the table, birthday cakes, holiday decorations—all the quiet rituals of a stable home.

That illusion lasted only until James opened the door before we had even knocked. As we approached, I scanned the windows—no curtain twitched, no shadow shifted. There were no signs of anyone waiting or watching. For a moment, I wondered if they had security cameras, but the longer I stood there, the more I sensed it wasn't surveillance that opened the door so quickly.

It was anticipation.

James towered over us—tall, broad, with thinning hair and soft, tired eyes. He smiled with a gentle distraction that invited trust without asking for anything in return. His presence made me want to smile back. There was something contagious about his quiet warmth, as though he had learned to be kind because life around him demanded it.

Then Salina appeared.

She was smaller than I expected—barely four feet eleven—with a slight limp that caused her to tilt as she walked, as if one side of her body lagged behind the other. Her voice was delicate, almost musical, and her sweetness was so perfectly pitched that refusing anything she offered felt almost offensive. Tea? Biscuits? She insisted with the polished hospitality of someone who had hosted hundreds of times yet never lost her script.

To an untrained eye, she looked maternal— fragile, even.

To me, she looked curated.

Her hands were always composed in her lap, fingertips lightly touching as if in prayer—or calculation. Every object she handled was placed with deliberate care, aligned with a precision that warned of consequences if anything in her domain fell out of order.

But it was her eyes that betrayed her.

Small. Black. Darting—like tadpoles trapped in a shallow puddle.

When James looked at her, she softened instantly, smiling with docile warmth. She touched Devin gently, spoke to him sweetly, doted on him as though he were her most beloved child.

But the moment James and Devin looked away, her expression dropped.

The softness vanished.

And those obsidian eyes turned on me—piercing, unblinking, calculating.

It wasn't anger.

It was recognition.

A silent message passed between us:

I see you. You don't belong here.

Something inside me tightened, and the illusion shattered. I saw her clearly then—what Devin must have grown up seeing: kindness as theater, affection as performance. A woman who had learned to weaponize gentleness with ruthless precision.

Salina had raised Devin to shrink.

She had kept him small—illiterate, underdeveloped, unsure of his own worth.

She denied him literacy, masking it as a form of praise.

"You don't need to learn, darling. You already know everything."

A sabotage veiled as nurturing.

Before James, she played the devoted mother—polished and perfect. But behind the mask, she crafted each crack in Devin's confidence. Every insecurity she instilled was a thread in the web she'd woven.

Salina's gaze never wavered as it locked onto mine.

I understood.

And she knew I understood.

Devin sat quietly—attempting to please her, trying to read her cues, unaware that doing so was impossible. Salina never intended to be content; contentment would have meant relinquishing control.

James, by contrast, was a man of few words. His silence wasn't calm—it was exhaustion. Years spent smoothing tensions, softening edges, and surviving under the rule of a woman whose moods dictated the temperature of their household had worn him down. He carried the stoop of a man who apologized for things that weren't his fault.

When he did speak, it was to defuse tension, to keep the peace, to steady the room. I later realized that this wasn't just his temperament—it was his survival instinct.

Salina's presence dominated everything. Even seated, she controlled the room—the scrape of a chair, the passing of a plate, the rise and fall of conversation. She spoke with gentle authority, her tone sweet enough to disguise the weight of her words. One wrong answer, and her warmth extinguished instantly.

"Remember," she would coo to Devin, "you are smart and intelligent."

But beneath that praise lay cruelty—because she engineered his dependence. She withheld literacy from him, ensuring he remained permanently reliant on her. This wasn't ignorance. It was a strategy of control disguised as love.

Miles, Devin's half-brother, was Salina's pride: polished, articulate, quick to charm. He had been raised in the warmth of her attention, while Devin grew up in its shadow. Miles drifted through short-lived jobs—painting, odd labor, the occasional contract—yet Salina celebrated his instability as ambition.

Devin, on the other hand, worked tirelessly at the same factory for decades, only to be dismissed as dull.

The patterns were clear.

When I hosted dinners, James arrived meek, polite, smiling, but speaking little. Before answering even simple questions, he would glance at Salina, as though seeking her permission.

Salina steered every interaction with such precision that recognizing her manipulation required effort. She interrupted lightly, redirected conversations, and subtly reminded everyone who held authority.

At restaurants—usually for James's birthday—Salina found fault with everything: the food, the service, the wine. It was never about taste. It was about control. Every complaint drew attention back to her, reclaiming the center she would never willingly share.

The first time I gave her a gift, she accepted it with a smile that didn't quite reach her eyes. Then she turned to Devin, hugging him and thanking him for the present, as if I hadn't even been there. I waited for her to correct herself.

She didn't.

And the gift vanished.

I never saw it again.

Merly, the daughter-in-law, acted as if she were an extension of Salina. When Merly stirred the pot, Salina pretended to disapprove, sighing dramatically and muttering that Merly was "bossing everyone around."

But in her eyes, there was satisfaction.

A satisfaction akin to an arsonist admiring the fire they've set.

Only later did I understand how carefully Salina engineered conflict. She stoked grievances behind closed doors, provoked rifts, and positioned herself as the mediator, all while tightening her control over everyone in the house. She isolated James, watched over him, never leaving him long enough to form honest connections.

In that house, nothing was left to chance.

Every word had purpose.

Every gesture was calculated, a move in a game none of us realized we were playing.

By the time I understood it, it was already too late.

The trap had been set long before I arrived—and Devin was ensnared in it, still believing it was love.

CHAPTER FOUR

❧

The Man Designed

Before anything else in this story can be understood—the manipulation, the cruelty, the small kingdom of control his family-built brick by brick—you have to understand Devin. Not the man he tried to become later, but the man they designed: the obedient son who stood in front of me the day we met, carrying years of invisible training in the slump of his shoulders and in the quiet way he waited for someone else to decide what came next.

From a distance, Devin could pass as inconspicuous—tall, soft-spoken, polite in the harmless way that makes strangers smile and forget him moments later. But up close, in the pauses between his sentences and the reflexive apologies he offered for things he hadn't done, the truth emerged.

He wasn't quiet by nature.

He had been shaped into silence.

Crafted by a mother who confused love with ownership.

Shaped by a father who surrendered his will long before Devin ever formed his own.

A man raised to doubt his perception—that was the first thing I learned about him.

Devin couldn't read, though he never recognized the word illiterate for what it meant. His mother had created a world where literacy wasn't necessary—only loyalty. She taught him that intelligence was a feeling, not a skill, and he believed her because she gave him no reason to question her authority.

I heard the scripts she fed him, spoken directly from his own mouth, recited like childhood hymns.

"You know I'm smart," he told me once, certain as gospel.

"My mum always said I was a clever boy."

The illusion shattered the day we filled out a form together. Devin held the pen like a child grips a crayon—too close to the tip, knuckles tight. He bent over the paper, as though proximity might steady the letters. Three minutes passed before he scrawled his name.

When he looked up, a triumphant, childlike smile spread across his face.

"There," he said proudly. "Perfect."

The signature was barely legible, climbing uphill like tired little hikers. But the pride in his eyes wasn't about the writing—it was about fulfilling the identity his mother had shaped for him: ability without effort, intelligence without change.

That was her cruelty.

She convinced him that there was no such thing as failure. It may sound kind, but the cost of never being allowed to grow is painfully clear.

People insulted him quietly—snide remarks drifting behind him like smoke. Devin rarely reacted. Cruelty slid off him as if he lived behind tempered glass. He wasn't immune; he simply didn't speak the language of humiliation.

One memory still unsettles me.

It didn't happen face-to-face. It arrived the way much of the cruelty in his life did—silently, through a screen.

Merly once texted Devin a single word:

Stupid.

No context. No explanation. Just that one word.

Devin stared at his phone, confusion flickering across his face—not shame. That, more than anything, disturbed me. He tapped the screen once and looked up.

"Is that for me?"

James glanced over briefly, then responded without hesitation, "She's joking, my son. Don't pay attention. Your mum says call her back instead."

And just like that, offense turned into instruction.

Cruelty became obedience.

Devin accepted it—not because he lacked dignity, but because he had been taught to interpret mistreatment as loyalty.

"That's my family," he would later say when I tried to name what I'd seen.

"That's my brother."

"That's my mum."

"That's Merly."

Each statement felt less like an explanation and more like a wall being built around his perception—a boundary he had been conditioned never to cross.

When I pushed back—when I challenged the message—the response escalated, again through text.

Miles intervened—not to deny the insult, but to reframe it.

He messaged Devin, claiming Merly hadn't meant anything by it.

"No," he wrote. "She just said to be careful. Because Devin is stupid."

Then, as if correcting himself mid-thought, he added:

"Because we know your kind. Not suggesting you are."

The words were careful. Calculated. Racially coded and deliberately vague. Not shouted. Not explicit. That was the point.

It was a language designed to wound while remaining defensible.

Merly hadn't called Devin stupid because she believed he lacked intelligence. She used the word because it served a function. It reinforced hierarchy. It justified speaking for him. It questioned his relationships. It cast me as a risk rather than a partner.

If Devin was "stupid," any independence he showed could be dismissed as manipulation by someone else—by me.

It wasn't an opinion.

It was a tactic.

Devin, trained from childhood to absorb contradiction without protest, accepted it without challenge. Praise and insult came from the same mouths. He had learned to treat both as proof of care.

That's how control survives.

Not through constant cruelty, but through brief, deniable moments of it—delivered softly enough to be explained away, often enough to shape behavior, and strategically enough to remind the target of their place.

Two architects raised him.

Salina was the designer—the strategist who weaponized praise and denied autonomy with quiet precision.

James was the enforcer—not through anger or violence, but through steady, unquestioning repetition.

"James," she once said when Devin was seventeen, "tell him he doesn't need college. He's not cut out for that."

James repeated her words verbatim.

"Listen to your mum. She knows what's right."

Another time, Devin saved enough money for a used car. He barely finished speaking before she dismissed him.

"You won't know how to handle that responsibility."

And James echoed, gently,

"No use arguing with her, lad. Best keep things simple."

Obedience wasn't taught.

It was inherited.

By the time I met him, Devin lived in a world meticulously crafted for him—an heirloom handed down, one he didn't know he could refuse. A world where independence was framed as recklessness, curiosity as troublemaking, and disagreement as betrayal.

Devin wasn't someone who ignored reality.

He was someone whose reality had been edited for him.

And long before I understood the machinery behind it—the manipulation, the coercion, the way his family spoke through him more than he spoke for himself—I understood him.

Not because he told me who he was.

But because his silence spoke louder than words.

On the other hand, whatever Miles did to him—the belittling, the small mocking jabs disguised as brotherly humor, the way he issued orders instead of requests—Devin accepted with reverent resignation.

"Oh, that's just my brother," he would murmur, sounding exactly like James when he spoke about Salina.

And whatever his mother inflicted on him— the dismissive wave of her hand when he tried to speak, the quiet sabotage she fed into daily life like poison dissolved in water—he forgave instantly, as if absolution were instinct rather than choice.

"My mum loves me," he'd insist, with a conviction that made my stomach flip.

He didn't say it defiantly, but with pride more than anything else—and that was hard to hear once I realized what was really going on.

Devin said it the way children recite prayers they were taught before they learned to question their meaning.

That, I learned, is what indoctrination looks like from the inside: devotion shaped so early and so deeply that cruelty feels routine, dismissal feels like affection, and abuse becomes indistinguishable from love.

Trying to rebuild a man who had been kept small was not going to be easy—that much was certain.

In the beginning, even the simplest attempts to help him grow felt like trying to rewire a maze someone else had designed. Convincing him to rethink his appearance was nearly impossible.

Grooming, clothing, basic presentation—it all struck him as unnecessary, even suspicious, because the idea of improving himself was foreign to the life he had been trained to live.

I remember the day I coaxed him into the salon.

Devin stood outside the door like someone preparing to walk into a courtroom.

"Just a trim," I said lightly. "Nothing more."

"I dunno."

"Come on. It'll be over before you know it."

He shook his head. "But my mum says there's nothing wrong with my hair."

"It's in your eyes, Devin."

"Yeah, but… it's fine. It's not like I can't see or anything."

"I know, but why not try something new?" I suggested. "How about you just give it a try once? If you don't like it, I won't say another word or ask you to do it again."

He shifted uncomfortably. Devin was extraordinarily uncertain—I could tell by the way his eyes kept flicking to the window, where he could see the stylists moving through the reflections of their own mirrors.

"Alright. Fine. I'll try it," he said reluctantly. "But only because you asked me to."

That would work. Still, I wanted him to want it too—I didn't want it to come across as a favor to me. In this case, though, I'd take any victory I could steal away from Salina.

When the cut was finished—clean lines and tight edges revealing a face finally visible beneath the overgrowth—the transformation was subtle but startling. He stared at himself in the mirror with a bewildered expression, as if the reflection belonged to another man entirely.

Devin lifted a hand to his face and touched it gently. It reminded me of a blind person feeling someone's face for the first time, trying to understand what they looked like.

"I look… different."

"You look like yourself," I said, "just with a new do." I chuckled a little to lighten the mood. Devin didn't.

For the first time, I saw something flicker across his features—a quiet lifting, an awakening, a sense of possibility slipping through the cracks of the life built around him.

Clothes came next: new jeans that fit him properly, a crisp shirt with structure, shoes that didn't look like they'd been inherited from someone else's adolescence.

With a fresh haircut and new duds, Devin stood a little taller. Maybe no one else could see it, but I could. He smiled differently, as if he were feeling something he hadn't allowed himself to feel before.

But when he showed his parents, the reaction was instant.

Salina's judgment passed over him and then darted away, like light turning from a mirror it didn't want to illuminate. Her jaw tightened. Her shoulders stiffened. The smile she forced was so brittle it looked as though it would crack if she opened her mouth too wide.

It wasn't just disapproval.

It was panic.

It was jealousy.

It was the horror of watching a puppet learn it might not need strings.

Every improvement he made loosened the framework she had spent decades constructing—the narrative that only Miles was capable, that only Miles was presentable, that only Miles was worth investing in.

The irony, sharp enough to draw blood, lay in how different Devin was at work. He was a man who functioned better than he lived. Away from the household that kept him small, he was sharpened. His movements were precise, his focus almost startling in its intensity.

Devin worked like a human printer—aligning labels, matching colors, and preparing products with near-mechanical consistency. He noticed imperfections others missed and adjusted gradients swiftly. The very tasks that demanded attention to detail, sequencing, and comprehension—skills his family insisted he lacked—were the ones he excelled at.

CHAPTER FIVE

Hooks

The first time I sat across from Salina at her kitchen table, I remember thinking the house felt embalmed rather than lived in. Not neglected—never that—but preserved. The air carried the faint aroma of lavender polish, masking something sour beneath it, as old fruit left too long in a bowl, quietly surrendering to rot.

The table was a shrine to order.

A lace cloth pressed flat into perfect submission.

Silver spoons aligned like soldiers.

A plate of untouched biscuits positioned dead center, waiting for guests who never seemed to come.

The house mirrored the table—old, but spotless. Every surface gleamed. Every corner had been accounted for. It wasn't a comforting cleanliness. It was oppressive—the handiwork of someone desperate to disguise disorder beneath shine.

For a woman who often insisted she was "slow" and "scatterbrained," Salina's meticulousness was unnerving. Even beneath the lace, I could see faint rings in the wood—ghosts of teacups long vanished.

Salina moved like someone who had rehearsed being watched. Her fingers glided from teapot to cup, pausing to straighten a doily that didn't need adjusting. Her wrists flexed with deliberate precision, every motion controlled, but her eyes never followed her hands.

Those glassy, unblinking eyes stayed fixed on me.

Measuring.

Learning.

Weighing.

"So," she said, voice sugary-sweet, "You're the new friend."

The way she said it made it clear this had been a topic in the house for days.

"Something like that," I replied, forcing a smile as the sour tang in the air made me instinctively brace.

Devin sat beside me like a child awaiting a scolding. His shoulders hunched, fingers nervously working at the edge of a napkin, his eyes staying low—refusing to meet either of ours. There was something unbearably boyish in his unease, like a punished child sitting through a lecture he'd heard before.

Salina's smile tightened, thin and gleaming like the edge of a paring knife.

"Devin doesn't bring many people around," she said.

I brushed a strand of hair from my face. "Yeah, well, I—"

"I wasn't finished, dear," she interrupted.

"Sorry… Salina."

"Yes, well, what I was saying is that if you're sitting here, that must mean you're special. Isn't that right, Devin?"

She delivered it like a compliment, but the warning underneath was obvious. The disdain in her voice was hard to miss. I wasn't sure if it was aimed at me, Devin, or the fact that we were a couple. Probably all three.

At the other end of the table, James chuckled faintly at the television, his attention divided. He didn't seem engaged with any of us, his laughter punctuating the silence intermittently. If not for his occasional chuckles, we might have forgotten he was there at all. When I glanced over, I'd find him absorbed in the screen—but every so often, his eyes would flick back to us, as if waiting for a signal from Salina.

Whenever she turned toward him, her entire demeanor softened. She poured his tea with an almost reverent touch, brushing his wrist gently as she asked if he was comfortable.

It was the portrait of a loving, devoted couple.

But when his eyes drifted back to the TV, the radiance vanished. What remained on her face was raw and chilling: calculation, contempt—something I couldn't yet articulate, but could feel deep in my bones.

Later that evening, as James shuffled toward his garage—his private refuge, I would soon learn—the smell of whiskey followed him down the hall. When the back door shut and his footsteps faded, Salina relaxed. The performance slipped a few millimeters.

That was when I saw it: the faint curl of satisfaction at the corner of her mouth. She wasn't waiting for his recovery.

She was waiting for his absence.

Salina leaned forward, elbows resting lightly on the lace, steam from her tea rising between us.

"You know," she began, glancing at Devin to confirm he was still within earshot, "Devin's... different. Always has been."

Her gaze slid back to me, testing.

"Different how?" I asked, keeping my tone neutral.

She smiled in that feline way of hers—teeth without warmth.

"Oh, just… not quite right somehow. He's slow. Always was. Never like Miles." Her posture relaxed at his name, then stiffened when she returned to Devin. "Miles has drive. Brains. He knows what he wants and knows how to get it." She tapped her fist lightly on the table, making the cups rattle.

"I see," was all I could manage.

"Take your elbows off the table, dear. It's not ladylike," Salina added, as if it were an afterthought, before returning seamlessly to her monologue. "My son Miles—you could tell from the moment he started school."

His name lingered in the air, like perfume she expected me to admire.

I was always mindful of etiquette; I knew better than to put my elbows on the table. But I did it subconsciously—perhaps as a quiet, rebellious reaction to her hostility. Maybe I was just tired, trying to relax in a place where relaxation wasn't permitted.

The silence stretched. The TV droned on in the background. After a moment, I broke it, deciding to ask.

"Why do you think Devin's different?" I said, almost lazily.

Her thin lips parted, as if she might laugh.

"I haven't the faintest idea," she said, with a practiced shrug. "He's not like me. Never was. Some children just… turn out wrong, I suppose."

She said it lightly, but it landed with weight.

The way she emphasized him made it sound as though even speaking his name disgusted her—or maybe it was another poisoned jab meant to keep him small. Either way, there was no version of that sentence that wasn't cruel.

Beside me, Devin didn't move. His jaw clenched once, then went slack. He stared down at the lace tablecloth, tracing its endless loops with his fingertip, as if following the pattern might make him disappear into it. He didn't look at her. He didn't look at me.

He just waited for her voice to pass over him like bad weather.

Salina leaned back, satisfied with the damage. She took a dainty sip of tea, setting her cup down with a soft click.

"Anyway," she continued, brushing an invisible crumb from the tablecloth, "you seem like a nice girl. I used to have an Asian friend when I was young. She was so sweet, so polite."

I forced a smile. "Oh, yeah?"

Her eyes lit up, pleased with my compliance.

"Yes," she said dreamily. "Her name was… oh, what was it… something with an L."

The pause stretched thin.

The fridge's motor hummed in the background, its low, clinical sound filling the room.

The overhead light trembled in her cup, its reflection fractured by the ripple of her hand.

I caught myself staring at that reflection.

She caught me noticing.

I nodded, as if interested, though every nerve in me felt pulled taut. It wasn't just what she said—it was how she said it.

"I bet you'd know the name," Salina quipped. "It was something with an oriental flair."

"Hm," I pretended to think.

If the situation hadn't been so tense, I would have pointed out that people don't really use that word anymore. Instead, I let it pass.

That strange, suffocating feeling settled in my chest again. Salina's world had sharp edges no one else could see, and we were already standing too close to them.

When Devin and I finally stepped out of the house that night, the air outside felt shockingly fresh.

I took several deep breaths, as though I could flush her presence from my lungs.

"Be safe," James called from the doorway. "Don't be strangers."

I turned back to wave. He still stood there, hand lifted. Salina was already retreating inside.

Devin walked beside me down the narrow street, his shoulders hunched, as though her eyes were still on his back. His hands were shoved deep into his pockets. The weak light from the house stretched halfway down the driveway before fading behind us.

For a long time, he said nothing.

His face appeared pale under the streetlight, the usual boyish softness replaced by something hollow. His eyes stayed fixed ahead. His boots scuffed against the gravel, and with each step, his shallow breaths were audible.

"Sorry about my family," he said eventually. "They're… nuts."

He tried to make it sound like a joke, but it fell flat.

"You don't need to apologize for any of that," I replied.

"She just... my mother..." He stopped walking, glanced back toward the house, and lowered his voice. "She talks like that sometimes. She's always been like that. Since I was a kid."

He said it like a confession from someone who no longer fully believed the gospel he'd been raised on.

We stopped beneath a streetlamp. His jaw tightened, as though chewing on whatever he wanted to say next.

"And your dad?" I asked quietly.

Devin let out a hollow laugh. "He believes her. They told us once—me and Miles—that they were a team. That no one could ever come between them." He kicked a pebble, sending it rolling down the road.

We started walking again, slower this time. I caught his reflection in the darkened windows we passed—his face thin, eyes empty in the glass.

I realized then that whatever Salina had taken from him, she hadn't done it all at once. She had chipped away quietly, piece by piece, until silence became the safest place he knew.

After that night, I began watching her more closely—the slight shifts in tone, the delicate choreography of her cruelty, how her voice softened whenever James entered the room, how her hand found his as if on cue, the devoted wife in her finest role. And the instant his attention drifted, the performance died. Her eyes—sharp, black, gleaming with cold satisfaction—cut straight to me, as if to remind me who the real audience was.

Salina never raised her voice.

She didn't need to.

Her power lived in the pauses, the small smile, the quiet rearranging of the truth.

And I saw, more clearly than ever, that Devin had never stood a chance.

Not in that house.

Not under "Mommy Dearest."

The phrase suited her.

In the weeks that followed, Salina lingered like a scent that wouldn't fade—from Devin's voice, from the air around us, from the tense stillness that settled whenever her name came up. She didn't need to be in the room to command it. Her absence felt as heavy as her presence.

Somewhere in that suffocating grip, I gave her a name:

The Devil in Disguise.

Because that's what she was. Not the kind of devil that storms into a room with rage and noise, but the kind that serves you tea with both hands, leaving you wondering—hours later—what exactly she took from you while you drank it.

What I didn't realize then was how little I understood of what she was capable of.

The Devil already had her hooks in Devin. And by standing next to him, I had quietly stepped into her line of sight.

CHAPTER SIX

Prisoner

Devin and I began dating a month after mid-2017. By the time I met his entire family, the rhythm of their world—already strange and uneven—shifted almost overnight. What had once been an uneasy quiet became a pattern of constant intrusion. Miles and his wife, Merly, started showing up whenever Devin visited his parents. At first, I thought it was a coincidence. But after several perfectly timed appearances, it became clear it was no accident.

It was orchestrated.

Whenever Devin called, Merly's sharp voice could often be heard in the background, telling him he was disturbing his father. James—Devin's father— grew increasingly muddled under her influence, struggling to form thoughts of his own, let alone defend his son. When Devin planned a visit, Salina intercepted the plan before it reached James. Suddenly, Miles and Merly were "coming for dinner" or "already on their way," and Devin was gently told to come another weekend instead.

Even the smallest details bore their control. The phone was left off the hook, messages went unanswered, and gifts quietly disappeared from shelves. Devin's presence was erased gradually, methodically. One of the first things to vanish was the cowhide rug Devin had proudly gifted them. After a month, it was simply gone—seemingly as if it had never existed at all.

Presence, in that house, was a privilege granted and revoked at will.

It wasn't until 2019 that the logic behind that system finally surfaced in words. Miles and Devin got into an argument about the house—the one Devin had grown up in and still considered his father's home. What started as a dispute about access soon revealed something far more disturbing.

Instead of confronting Devin face-to-face, Miles chose to send a message.

In it, he told Devin that he owed his life to him.

Not as an emotional outburst.

Not as a metaphor.

As a statement of fact.

Miles claimed that Devin existed because he had needed him—that Salina had another child not out of love or a desire for a family, but because Miles required support: financial, practical, permanent. According to him, Devin had been brought into the world to serve a purpose—to justify a marriage, to secure stability, to create something Miles could always draw from.

Then came the final claim:

Miles told him the house should be his, that it had always been meant for him. That Devin had no rightful claim to it at all.

The implication was chilling.

Devin was not born to be wanted. He was born to be useful.

Devin read the message in silence. The familiar reflex to apologize surfaced immediately—years of conditioning urging him to absorb blame, to smooth over words that should never have been spoken. But something faltered this time. The message named what he had felt his entire life but had never been able to articulate.

The argument escalated, folding into entitlement and ownership—who belonged, who mattered, who had the right to remain. Miles spoke with the certainty of someone who believed the ending had already been written. In his mind, the house was not James's. It was a resource already allocated.

And Devin—quiet, obedient Devin—was reminded of his role.

Not as a son.

Not as family.

But as a means.

That understanding followed me into a lunch at the house Devin and I had moved into together some time later. We were seated at the table, and the conversation drifted aimlessly. I spoke without fully considering the consequences. I told them—plainly—that Miles had texted Devin, claiming Devin owed him his life. Miles had said that Devin existed because he had needed him, and that James—Devin's father—had been drawn into a marriage that served that purpose. Miles also said the house should be his.

For the first time since I had known her, Salina's composure cracked. Her eyes widened, sharp and exposed, but she said nothing. Not a word. Not a denial. Not even a deflection.

James's reaction was quieter. He lowered his gaze to the table, his shoulders folding inward, as though the weight of the words had pressed him down. He didn't argue. He didn't ask what I meant.

He looked embarrassed.

The silence that followed was deliberate. No one corrected me. No one challenged the account. The truth sat between us, unspoken but unmistakably present.

From then on, the erasure intensified.

Whenever we dropped by unannounced, the mantel told its own story. Photographs of Devin had been replaced by framed pictures of Miles and Merly—wedding photos, holidays, carefully curated reminders of who now occupied the center of the family narrative.

James never seemed to notice. Salina had quietly reshaped the house, remaking it in the image of the family she preferred rather than the one she had.

Miles embodied everything Salina had once tried to force Devin to be: confident, articulate, and skilled in the delicate art of charm. He possessed the polish that misled others into confusing arrogance with warmth. Beneath the surface, however, was a sharp calculation—a constant evaluation of weakness and opportunity.

And then there was Merly.

If Miles was the hand guiding the pieces, Merly was the voice declaring every move—louder, bolder, and entirely unapologetic in her disdain. From the start, she made no effort to hide her dislike for me. Her compliments, when they did come, were delayed, landing like punches disguised as praise.

We met only once in person, yet her presence lingered in James's house like a stain that refused to fade. Her voice filled rooms even when she wasn't there—carried through whispers, repeated conversations, and carefully shaped stories that always circled back to me.

"Oh, she's still around?" someone would say, echoing her mocking tone.

"She really is something, isn't she?" another would add, laughing nervously, unaware they were simply repeating lines fed to them.

The stories were never kind. They were engineered to undermine, isolate, and mark me as an outsider. Once, Merly even boasted to Devin that she would run a background check on me, as though decency required vetting. I laughed it off at the time. Later that night, it replayed in my mind until sleep became impossible.

Miles and Merly understood the system they were operating within. Together, they honed the same machinery Salina had built decades earlier: isolation disguised as concern, control masquerading as family loyalty. While not as subtle as Salina, their intent was the same.

Calls to James were intercepted or sent straight to voicemail. Visits were carefully monitored. Gifts Devin brought—wine, fruit baskets, small tokens—disappeared within days, replaced by cheaper alternatives from Miles, with his name neatly inscribed on the card.

I watched Devin's hope diminish in increments. He would call his father only to be told James was "busy," or that Miles and Merly were already there. Salina's explanations were always gentle, always sweet.

"Oh, you know how forgetful he is…"

"We just thought it would be safer this way…"

It was never about forgetfulness.

It was never about safety.

It was about control.

The pattern was unmistakable—the same soft deceit, the same deliberate erosion of confidence. Salina had built the mold; her son and his wife perfected it.

They didn't need to shout or accuse.

They only needed to whisper, tightening the walls inch by inch until Devin could no longer tell where family ended and captivity began.

He was a prisoner among kin.

And the most devastating part wasn't the confinement itself but how normal it felt to him. Devin had been raised to believe that love meant endurance, loyalty meant silence, and that questioning his place was the ultimate betrayal.

People raised in emotional captivity don't fear losing their freedom.

They fear losing their captors.

And by the time I understood this fully, I realized I wasn't just standing beside a man trapped by his family—

I was standing on the same battlefield.

The Devil had already hooked him.

And by loving him, I too had placed myself within reach.

CHAPTER SEVEN

The Quiet Countdown

It was sometime in 2019 when Salina, with the same offhand tone one might use to comment on the weather, mentioned that she and Merly had already arranged James's funeral—while he was still very much alive. She said it between sips of tea, her eyes bright, almost amused, as though death were simply a date penciled neatly into her calendar.

For a moment, I thought I must have misheard her. Surely no one could speak so casually about the death of their own husband. But she meant it. Every word. There was a calm certainty in her voice that sent a cold shiver through me, a quiet satisfaction that made my skin prickle.

I didn't respond.

I couldn't.

I glanced at Devin, waiting for shock, for outrage, for any sign of life at all. He didn't look up. His eyes stayed fixed on the floor, his silence automatic, practiced. It struck me then that this wasn't the first time he'd heard her speak this way. He had learned long ago that resistance only made things worse.

That silence spoke louder than any confession ever could.

It wasn't disbelief that held him still.

It was a surrender.

In that moment, I saw the full extent of Salina's control. She didn't need to raise her voice or issue commands. Her power lived in subtler places—in the finality of her tone, in the confidence with which she spoke, as though outcomes were already decided.

What stunned me most was how easily the room absorbed her words. No one questioned her. No one challenged the assumption that James's death was inevitable—and imminent. James himself, sitting in the next room, remained unaware that his funeral had already been planned without him.

It became clear that Salina didn't merely manage her family.

She controlled it.

From the beginning, I had sensed the quiet anticipation that flickered between Salina and Miles whenever James's name was mentioned. They spoke of him as though he already had one foot planted firmly in the afterlife.

At one point, Salina told me—almost cheerfully—that "James isn't well, you know. The doctors think it's bowel cancer."

There was no fear in her voice. No grief. Only a strange brightness in her eyes that unsettled me more than the words themselves.

It was the look of someone already counting down the days.

Not long after, James let something slip— almost accidentally, as though he hadn't meant to say it at all. He mentioned that Miles held the house documents.

Devin froze. He hadn't known. He stared at his father, disbelief thick in the silence between them. In that moment, the pattern finally locked into place: the inheritance, the house, the quiet campaign that had been unfolding for years beneath the guise of concern.

When I turned toward Salina, she busied herself with the table—straightening papers, smoothing fabric, doing anything to appear detached from a decision that had already been made.

By 2023, the betrayal in that household had curdled into something unrecognizable—an infection that seeped into every conversation, every pause, every moment Devin tried to breathe freely.

The breaking point came with a wound on James's leg.

What started as a gash spiraled into severe bleeding and infection with alarming speed. When James was admitted to the hospital, the medical team struggled to explain it. Doctors couldn't identify a clear cause. Tests ruled out the usual explanations—trauma, vascular injury, infection—typical of age or lifestyle. One specialist mentioned the possibility of a rare condition, something scarcely seen anymore, a disease so uncommon it was largely absent from modern medical practice.

Even then, no one could say for certain.

James relayed this to us in fragments, his voice thin and uneven, as if repeating information he barely understood. He told us that Merly had been with him when the wound first appeared. She had initially tended to it, applying medicated cream directly to the bleeding skin. Whether it had been done improperly or the wound worsened on its own, no one could determine.

What lingered was not an explanation but an absence of one.

While James was hospitalized, still feverish and disoriented, he let something slip that chilled me. He said Merly and Miles had instructed him not to believe a word we told him. His medical contacts had already been changed. Merly and Miles' names had replaced Devin's on his emergency paperwork.

Even the nurses struggled to understand who Devin was in relation to him.

After that, Miles and Merly's presence intensified, moving through the situation with the ease of people who believed authority had already shifted.

Miles carried himself with effortless polish—his voice calm, his confidence assumed—while Devin, standing beside him, seemed to recede into the background.

The comparison was never explicit, but it lived in every exchange: Miles framed as capable and decisive, Devin as uncertain and expendable.

Salina watched it all with unsettling stillness.

She allowed Devin's drinking and marijuana use to continue unchecked, almost as though she were observing an experiment she expected to collapse under its own weight. She never suggested help. Never intervened. She waited.

But he didn't fail.

With relentless effort, Devin quit drinking. The process was slow and brutal, but he clawed his way back to clarity. A few years later, he stopped using marijuana as well. He regained full control over his mind, his habits, his future—something that should have inspired relief or pride.

Instead, when Salina found out, the room around her seemed to freeze.

She offered no congratulations. No relief. No warmth. Her face remained carefully blank, as though the good news had arrived for the wrong person.

Years earlier, shortly after Devin and I began building our life together, I told his parents that I was helping him improve his reading and writing skills. His father expressed his gratitude with a sincerity that touched his eyes.

But his mother—she didn't even acknowledge me.

Her gaze slid past me, as though even recognizing my presence would concede something she wasn't willing to face.

And in that moment, it became clear what had truly unsettled her.

My presence had disrupted something much deeper.

I had unwittingly interfered with a quiet, long-standing strategy—one that had been carefully designed to weaken Devin, to sever the bond between father and son, and to keep him dependent and diminished.

They weren't just positioning themselves for James's assets.

They were also positioning themselves for Devin's.

Miles and Merly had set their sights on what Devin owned: his home, his stability. Salina's interest ran even deeper—toward his superannuation, the future she believed she still controlled.

Every manipulation began to align. Every lie. Every subtle push toward self-destruction.

It hadn't been random.

It had been deliberate.

Now that Devin was growing stronger, they could feel their grip slipping.

Salina's expression that day told me everything. Beneath her stillness was silent rage—the fury of a woman watching decades of control begin to fracture.

From that point on, I documented everything: conversations, offhand remarks, and passive-aggressive comments masked as concern. I stopped relying solely on memory.

I began to see the structure of the quiet war within that family: affection wielded as control, smiles concealing hidden motives, and praise twisted into something toxic.

This was not chaos.

It was a strategy.

In that house, there were generals, soldiers, and casualties.

Devin—the son they had shaped but never intended to free—was never meant to escape it.

CHAPTER EIGHT

The Polished Son

It was early 2018 when I first met Miles—the polished son, the one Salina always measured Devin against, even when she pretended not to.

We met at Devin's house one quiet afternoon. His parents weren't there. Just the three of us, and the atmosphere felt slightly compressed, as though the walls themselves were holding their breath.

Miles arrived without warning.

The door opened, and the small space seemed to shrink. He stepped inside with a confidence that didn't ask permission. Tall and neatly dressed in a crisp button-down that looked out of place against the cluttered simplicity of Devin's home, he carried himself like someone accustomed to being observed—and admired.

"Hey, bro," Miles said, clapping Devin lightly on the shoulder. "Didn't know you had company."

Devin startled, then smiled too quickly. "Oh—yeah. This is—this is her."

Miles turned to me and extended his hand. His grip was firm, practiced.

"So," he said, pleasant but sharpened at the edges, "you're with Devin now."

It wasn't a question. It was a statement wrapped in politeness.

"Yes," I replied.

His eyes lingered a second longer than necessary, scanning, measuring, filing something away. I felt it immediately—the sensation of being assessed, not socially but strategically.

"Good," he said lightly. "He needs someone."

Devin laughed, uncertain. "Miles is just—he worries."

"I do," Miles agreed smoothly. "Someone has to."

That was my first glimpse of how he positioned himself—not as a brother, but as a supervisor.

Miles drifted through the room, glancing at the taped blankets over the windows, the crowded table, and the sink still holding remnants of a meal. His face didn't register surprise or discomfort. There was no reaction at all.

That absence spoke volumes.

This was exactly how Miles expected Devin to live.

"Well," Miles said, turning back to us, "I just wanted to check in. Make sure everything's… fine."

He smiled when he said it. A friendly smile. A public smile.

"Everything's fine," Devin said quickly.

"Good," Miles replied. "Mum worries."

Of course she did.

When he left, the air shifted again, expanding slightly, as though the house had exhaled.

"That was my brother," Devin said, unnecessarily.

"I know," I replied.

He didn't ask what I meant.

After that first meeting, something changed.

Every time I visited Devin's house, there were signs—subtle at first, easy to overlook if you didn't know what you were seeing. A chair was knocked slightly out of place. A mug shattered in the sink. A cupboard door is hanging loose on one hinge.

"What happened here?" I asked once, taking in the kitchen.

Devin hesitated. "Miles came by."

"And?"

"We had a fight."

About what?

He wouldn't say.

It happened again. And again.

Each visit brought a new trace—cushions displaced, the living room rearranged by force rather than habit, the air thick with something unresolved. Devin would tidy quickly, nervously, as if erasing evidence might erase the conflict itself.

Then I noticed the marks on him.

The first was a shallow cut beneath his cheekbone.

"What happened to your face?" I asked.

He flinched. "It's nothing."

"It's a cut."

"Just an accident."

Accidents don't repeat themselves with this kind of precision.

Soon, there were scratches on his arms. A bruise near his wrist.

One evening, I took his hand and gently turned it toward the light.

"This isn't normal," I said. "You don't keep getting hurt like this by chance."

He pulled his hand away, jaw tight. "Please. Don't."

That was when I stopped asking and started insisting.

"You're not protecting anyone by staying quiet," I said. "And you're not protecting yourself either."

He sat in silence for a long time, staring at the floor, shoulders slumped, as though bracing for punishment that hadn't yet arrived.

Finally, he spoke.

"He keeps picking fights," Devin said quietly.

"About what?"

His voice dropped. "About you. About us."

I waited.

"He says I've changed," Devin continued. "That I think I'm better than him now. That Dad listens to me more. That I don't come around as I used to."

"And then?" I asked.

Devin swallowed. "I snapped."

"What did you say?"

He lifted his gaze, eyes weary, stripped of their usual reflexive defense.

"I asked him," Devin said quietly, ""Why are you fighting me? Is it because I found a good woman?"

The words hit us both like a weight.

"And?" I asked.

"He snapped," Devin said. "He got furious. Really furious."

That was the turning point.

Not a misunderstanding—but the beginning of a war.

It took me some time to understand the root of it.

Miles wasn't confused by Devin's relationship with me.

He was threatened by it.

Because I wasn't just a partner—I was proof.

Proof that Devin could grow. That he could make choices. That he could step beyond the narrow role his family had assigned him. And worse—proof that James, his stepfather, might start seeing him differently.

Miles needed to be superior. Not just better—but seen as better.

Especially in James's eyes.

Miles had built his identity on that position: the capable son, the polished one, the man who could be trusted, admired, and deferred to. Devin's progress disrupted that hierarchy. Each step Devin took forward felt like a subtraction from Miles's standing.

It wasn't a rivalry.

It was fear.

Miles carried Salina's envy like a legacy—her resentment, her need to dominate, her intolerance for anything that disrupted the order she'd so carefully crafted.

Devin's happiness wasn't merely inconvenient.

It was unforgivable.

We saw Miles again a few months later at a local pub, where Salina and James were celebrating their birthdays. The room buzzed with chatter and clinking glasses, but our table carried a strange stillness, tension threaded beneath the noise.

James sat at the end of the table, shoulders rounded, hands cupped around his drink. He smiled when spoken to, nodded when nodded at—a man who had learned that silence was safer than opinion.

Salina sat upright beside him, composed and observant. She surveyed the table like a director before opening night, ensuring everyone was positioned exactly where she wanted them.

Miles sat comfortably, spine straight, movements fluid. He cut his food carefully, each bite measured.

Devin, by contrast, leaned over his plate, gripping his fork awkwardly, eating quickly, as though the food might disappear if he didn't finish in time.

Salina reached over and patted his arm. "Remember, Devin," she said warmly, loud enough for the table to hear, "You're smart. You're intelligent. Don't ever forget that."

Devin beamed. "I know, Mum."

Her eyes flicked to Miles, approval unmistakable.

"Miles has always had such drive," she added. "He knows what he wants."

Miles smiled modestly. "I just try my best."

James raised his glass. "To family."

"To family," Miles echoed smoothly, holding his stepfather's gaze just a second longer than necessary.

"To family," Devin said last, his glass wobbling slightly in his hand.

I watched the choreography unfold. One son presented as capable, reliable, and impressive. The other reassured, praised, kept close—but never elevated.

Salina's praise for Devin was affectionate but limiting. It wrapped him in warmth while quietly denying him power.

She didn't empower him.

She contained him.

When we left the pub, the night air felt cooler, sharper. Devin walked beside me in silence, shoulders slumped.

"He's different," I said gently.

He laughed softly, embarrassed. "Of course he is. Miles—Mum made sure he was taught everything. School stuff. Rules. Life."

"And you?" I asked.

He hesitated.

"She said I was autistic," he said, his voice softer now. "But she loved me. She just... wasn't able to teach me properly. She said I didn't need all that."

His gaze met mine, a flicker of uncertainty crossing his face.

"She always told me I was smart. Intelligent. And I believed her. I really did."

"I know," I whispered back.

He stopped in his tracks, his shoulders slumping slightly.

"I believed her," he said, voice barely audible.

And in that moment, everything became painfully clear.

This wasn't favoritism.

It was designed.

One son polished, trained, and prepared to represent.

The other kept soft, dependent, and convinced he was complete, while being denied the tools to stand on his own.

Both were shaped deliberately.

Miles was taught to shine.

Devin was taught to stay.

Standing beside him under a streetlight that illuminated every line of uncertainty on his face, I understood something essential:

This wasn't about love.

It was engineering.

And the tragedy wasn't that Devin hadn't seen it yet.

It was that he had been raised never to question it.

CHAPTER NINE

Silence at My Table

A few months later, once Devin and I had settled into a rhythm of our own, I invited his parents to dinner at my home.

Not because it was a special occasion.

But because I needed to see them on neutral ground.

Somewhere where the walls didn't belong to them, and the air didn't tilt in their favor. Somewhere, their quiet authority couldn't dictate the atmosphere simply by existing.

When they arrived, Salina wore her usual practiced smile—tight, polite, impenetrable. It was the smile she used when she wanted to appear agreeable without yielding an inch.

James followed a step behind her, shoulders rounded, hands clasped together as if he were entering a courtroom instead of a dining room. He nodded at me, offered a faint smile, and waited—always waited—for Salina to move first.

We sat down.

At first, I didn't understand what I was witnessing.

I thought James was shy.

Or tired.

Or simply being polite.

But something felt off—subtle, unsettling in a way I couldn't name yet.

He sat at my table, hands folded, elbows tucked, body contained. He chewed slowly, eyes lowered, shoulders hunched. Every question I asked seemed to float across the table, dissolving before it reached him.

"How have things been, James?"

A small nod.

"Everything okay at home?"

A faint shrug.

Sometimes, nothing—just silence, as if the act of answering had been disabled.

Across from him sat Salina.

Watching.

Monitoring.

Occupying the space around her as though she owned it, even though it wasn't her house.

Every time I addressed James directly, the muscles around Salina's mouth tightened—just barely, but unmistakably. She didn't need to interrupt with words. Her presence was the command.

The message was silent, but perfectly clear:

He speaks when I allow it.

At the time, I mistook it for awkwardness—maybe nerves, maybe unfamiliarity. I stayed polite, patient, unaware of the psychology unfolding before me.

But later, the truth hit with force.

Salina was insecure.

Deeply, terribly.

My presence threatened the world she had meticulously crafted.

It wasn't just that Devin had found a partner.

It was that he had found stability.

Someone who could lift him.

Someone who could help him grow.

Someone who might show James another version of his son.

A better one.

A more confident one.

A son worthy of pride.

And that could not be allowed.

If James began to see Devin differently—see him improving, learning, standing taller—then Salina's control would crack. Her narrative would weaken. The hierarchy would shift.

So, she made sure—absolutely sure—that James would never warm to me. Never feel close to me. Never truly knew who I was.

She needed to keep us strangers.

That night, sitting at my table, I saw the beginnings of it—even if I didn't yet fully understand.

Partway through dinner, I tried again, gently.

"James, would you like some more roast?"

He opened his mouth, just a fraction—a spark of response forming.

Before a single word escaped, Salina placed her hand on his arm.

Stillness.

James froze, his mouth closing. His gaze dropped to his plate.

"No, he's fine," Salina answered.

Her tone wasn't rude; it didn't need to be.

It carried the confidence of someone who had answered for him for decades.

My stomach tightened.

Devin shifted beside me, uneasy, sensing the tension without fully understanding it. He glanced between us, then back down at his plate.

And then, it clicked.

James's silence wasn't accidental.

It had been shaped.

Taught.

Enforced.

A silence forged to replace a voice long ago.

After dinner, Devin suggested we sit in the living room and watch a movie. He fumbled with the remote, eager to please, scrolling through titles until he found one that was familiar, safe.

"Dad likes this one," he said quietly, as though convincing himself.

James settled into the couch, his posture loosening for the first time that evening. When the movie began, I noticed a subtle change—his face softened, his eyes brightened. He leaned forward slightly, engaged, quietly enjoying what he was watching.

It was the most alive I had seen him all night.

Salina noticed too. Almost immediately, she shifted closer and placed her left leg over his—

Not casually.

Not absent-mindedly.

Deliberately.

The movement was slow and unmistakable. Possessive. Intimate in a way that made the air feel thick.

I froze.

The shock wasn't just that she did it—it was where and when: in front of other people. In front of her son. In front of me.

An elderly woman asserting ownership through physical dominance—reminding everyone in the room exactly where authority resided.

James stiffened slightly but didn't move away. His brief moment of enjoyment vanished. His body folded back into itself, smaller again, contained.

Devin didn't react.

He didn't even seem to notice.

That, somehow, disturbed me most of all.

Salina knew he wouldn't.

She knew Devin was too conditioned, too slow to register the nuance of what was happening. She counted on it. Her control thrived in spaces where no one challenged her, because no one recognized the behavior for what it was.

The movie played on, but the moment lingered like static in the room. I sat rigid on the couch, hyperaware, my mind racing.

This wasn't affection.

It was control.

A reminder.

James had been enjoying something without her approval—and she had reclaimed control the only way she knew how.

Without words.

Later, when the credits rolled, they stood to leave.

James moved slowly, carefully.

Salina was brisk and decisive.

At the door, she thanked me politely, her smile returning as though nothing unusual had happened.

Once they were gone, Devin exhaled.

"That went okay," he said, hopeful.

I looked at him—really looked at him—and felt the weight of what he couldn't see.

"That wasn't normal," I said gently.

He frowned. "What wasn't?"

I shook my head. "Nothing. We'll talk later."

He accepted that easily. Too easily.

That night, lying awake, I replayed the evening in my mind. The silence. The hand on James's arm. The leg draped possessively over his.

What I had witnessed wasn't awkwardness.

It wasn't age.

It wasn't a habit.

It was control disguised as care.

And for the first time, I understood just how deeply Salina's control ran—not just over her sons, but over her husband as well.

That dinner wasn't uncomfortable.

It was calculated.

There were other moments—quieter ones—that only made sense in hindsight.

Whenever James came to Devin's house to help with something—fixing a hinge, carrying tools, checking the car—he almost always arrived with Salina. But she never came inside. She stayed in the garage, sitting in the car or standing just beyond the doorway, arms folded, eyes scanning, waiting. She never commented on the filth Devin had been living in at the time—the clutter, the grime, the neglect. It never seemed to trouble her at all.

James didn't question it. He would step inside, do what he came to do, and leave again without remark—his silence rehearsed, his acceptance automatic. The condition of his son's home had been quietly normalized, absorbed into the same unspoken agreement that governed everything else.

At the time, I didn't understand it.

I remember watching her from the doorway once, noticing how deliberately she avoided crossing the threshold, keeping herself physically separate from Devin's space. I assumed it was discomfort, impatience, or simply preference.

I didn't yet understand that it wasn't avoidance.

It was a restraint.

Salina could tolerate her son living in squalor. What she could not bear was stepping into something that belonged to him.

Devin's house was proof of independence—fragile, imperfect. It represented ownership, autonomy, a life not entirely under her control. And she could not bear to inhabit it, even briefly.

James had been conditioned to accept this without question, to believe it was normal. That where his son lived was "fine," and that nothing was wrong enough to warrant concern.

But now, looking back, the meaning is unmistakable.

She wasn't indifferent.

She was jealous.

And jealousy, in her world, was not expressed through confrontation—but through absence.

It revealed exactly who held power, who was allowed to speak, and who had learned—over decades—that silence was survival.

It was the moment I realized that Devin hadn't just grown up in that environment.

He had been shaped by it.

And so had his father.

CHAPTER TEN

The Shadow Among Us

For a long time, I didn't understand why they were so aggressively against me.

That part, in hindsight, almost makes me laugh.

At the time, though, it was genuinely confusing.

Devin was not, by any conventional measure, the kind of man a family would hold up with pride. He was illiterate. He lived in a house so neglected it felt closer to a shelter than a home. He drank too much. He relied heavily on marijuana to numb the edges of a life he'd never been taught to manage.

And yet, they reacted to me as though I had swooped in to steal some prized bachelor—some man of wealth, status, and endless prospects. The accusations whispered behind my back painted me as a gold digger, a manipulator, a woman "after something."

The irony was absurd.

Sometimes, it genuinely made me laugh.

What exactly did they think I was digging for?

At the time, I assumed it was a projection, paranoia, or Salina's insecurity flaring at the idea of another woman influencing her son. I hadn't seen the full picture yet.

Now I do.

All their eyes were on him—not because of who Devin was then, but because of who he could become and what he quietly possessed.

Merly saw the family's weaknesses immediately:

An alcoholic father whose voice had been dulled by decades of submission,

A son numbing himself with alcohol and marijuana,

A mother who sabotaged her own child while calling it protection.

Where others might have seen dysfunction, Merly saw opportunity.

By the time I met her, I already sensed there were undercurrents in Devin's family I couldn't fully see. I had learned to recognize tension, manipulation, and silence disguised as peace. But nothing prepared me for Merly.

Our first—and only—face-to-face encounter happened at the opening of her car-cleaning business. Miles had invited us casually:

"Come down," he'd said. "Say hello. See what we're building."

It was framed as friendly, supportive, and family-minded.

The moment I stepped inside, the air shifted.

Merly stood behind the counter, her posture sharp, phone in hand. Her smile was polite but cold—the kind offered out of obligation rather than interest. When Miles introduced us, she gave me a brief glance, just enough to acknowledge my presence, then returned her attention to her screen.

"This is Devin's partner," Miles said.

Merly didn't look up.

"Hi," she said, her tone flat.

That was it.

No handshake. No question. No warmth.

She dismissed me without ceremony, as if I were an interruption rather than a guest.

Later, Devin leaned in and whispered, "She's just busy."

Busy people acknowledge others; dismissive people don't.

That was our only direct interaction, yet from that moment, Merly began working quietly behind the scenes.

Devin later told me she had been "asking about me" even before we met.

"What kind of asking?" I asked.

He shrugged. "Just... questions."

But she never asked me directly—she didn't need to.

Merly gathered information like a seasoned manipulator—through casual comments, loaded questions, and subtle observations.

"She seems intense."

"Does she work?"

"She's very confident, isn't she?"

Always said lightly.

Always said to Salina.

Always said when Devin wasn't in the room.

And James—silent James—sat at the center of it all, his judgment dulled by alcohol, his instincts overridden by Salina's authority.

In that fog, Merly planted her seeds.

By the time I understood what was happening, the narrative had already taken shape.

"She's not right for him."

"She's after something."

"She's trouble."

These comments were never spoken directly to me.

Never confronted openly.

Always whispered.

Always framed as concern.

Devin didn't see it.

How could he?

He had been raised to trust the women in his family without question. His mother's word had always been law. He couldn't imagine that someone inside the family—someone married into it—could be quietly undermining him.

And Salina allowed it.

Encouraged it.

Because by then, something else was happening.

Devin was improving.

He was drinking less.

Thinking more clearly.

Standing taller.

Speaking with more confidence.

And Salina hated it.

I sensed her jealousy long before I could articulate it. Every improvement Devin made unsettled her. She avoided us when we visited James's house, suddenly "out," suddenly "busy," and nowhere to be found.

We'd arrive, and James would look both relieved and nervous.

"She's not home," he'd say quietly.

Later, I understood it wasn't a coincidence.

She didn't want to cross paths with me.

She didn't want to see Devin thriving under someone else's influence.

But everything changed after she saw me publicly, after the business opening.

Not long after that encounter, Miles and Merly moved back into James's house.

The timing wasn't random.

The territory had to be reclaimed.

That was Merly's move.

Merly hadn't grown up in the family the way Devin and Miles had, but she understood power. She knew how to observe, how to wait, how to position herself.

She saw a family ruled by silence and hierarchy.

She saw a mother desperate to retain control.

She saw two sons raised in competition—one polished, one diminished.

And she saw Devin as a tool.

Not a person.

A tool.

His house.

His independence.

His financial security.

His future.

Miles was waiting for his stepfather's house, for inheritance, for validation that never fully arrived.

Devin already had what Miles wanted, and that imbalance festered.

The accusations against me—suddenly, they made sense.

They weren't protecting Devin from me.

They were guarding their access to him.

As Devin rebuilt his life, the atmosphere grew more hostile. Each step he took toward independence destabilized the narrative Merly had carefully crafted, where she was the helpful daughter-in-law, the caring one, the sensible voice guiding James and Salina.

Behind that image, Merly relentlessly worked to dismantle what Devin and I were building.

"She's changing you," she told him, according to Devin.

"How?" he asked.

"You're not the same anymore."

He paused. "I think that's the point."

The silence afterward told him everything.

By the time I fully understood Merly's intentions, she had perfected her mask. In public, she was dutiful. Supportive. Concerned. She was also visibly active in a born-again church community— always present at gatherings, quick to quote scripture, eager to project an image of faith and morality. To anyone watching, she appeared devout, grounded, morally anchored.

But it didn't take long to notice that her devotion was selective. The relationships she cultivated mirrored the ones she built elsewhere: purposeful, transactional, useful. The church wasn't a sanctuary—it was a network. A place to form business connections, secure goodwill, and reinforce the image she needed others to believe. Faith, like everything else in her life, was something to be worn when it served her and discarded when it didn't.

In private, she was corrosive.

Her hatred wasn't loud. It didn't need to be.

It lived in suggestions, omissions, and strategic concern.

She didn't want Devin destroyed outright. She wanted him weakened, dependent, easier to manage.

Because a strong Devin threatened everything: Miles's sense of superiority, Salina's control, and Merly's access to a security she could never manufacture on her own.

This wasn't love. It was an acquisition.

And once I saw it, I understood something chilling:

Merly hadn't entered the family by accident. She had chosen it.

And now, she was determined to reshape it— no matter who she had to erode in the process.

CHAPTER ELEVEN

Gifts and Poison

As Devin grew up, Salina perfected the same strategy with him.

She gave gifts that were cheap in substance but wrapped to appear expensive.

The presentation was always deliberate: glossy paper, carefully tied ribbons, boxes chosen for effect—just enough to convince James that his son was being generously provided for.

In reality, the gifts never changed. Inexpensive T-shirts. Hoodies. Bed sheets. Twenty or thirty dollars at most. Items chosen not out of care or meaning, but for appearance.

I watched James's face light up every time. He believed the illusion.

He believed his son was cherished, well looked after, never lacking.

Devin smiled too, trained early to be grateful for whatever was placed in his hands.

Salina and Merly had a particular talent: they could turn even the simplest acts of care into weapons.

Every gift Devin and I gave to his parents— whether a bottle of wine, a small household item, or a thoughtful voucher—was subtly undermined, overshadowed, or erased. What should have been gestures of connection became arenas for jealousy and sabotage.

It began years earlier, in what had seemed like an innocent family arrangement at the time.

Devin booked a Groupon hotel deal for his parents' holiday to a regional area. Merly insisted on coming along so the family could stay together. Miles approved the plan and assured Devin that they would reimburse him. I made the booking using Devin's card.

The moment they checked in, James rang to say that Salina was unhappy with the room.

At the same time, Miles and Merly began texting Devin, complaining that the hotel was "too expensive" and refusing to pay their share. I later checked the accommodation—it was a standard Quest hotel, and the Groupon deal had already cut the price significantly.

After the holiday, Salina told us that Merly had accused me of pocketing money from the booking through my business account. According to her, the hotel was far too expensive for what it was. The accusation seemed outlandish.

It took over a year for Miles and Merly to finally reimburse Devin. At the time, I didn't yet realize that Salina and Merly were already working closely together. Looking back, it's clear: this wasn't confusion or ignorance—it was deliberate manipulation.

Despite all of this, Devin continued giving gifts to his parents for every birthday, Christmas, and special occasion.

The pandemic in 2020 intensified everything.

Miles and Merly stayed almost constantly at James's house, restricting visits under the guise of protecting him from COVID. When Devin dropped off birthday gifts in July 2020, Miles confronted us aggressively at the gate.

"I'm protecting my parents," he said.

Salina said nothing. Her silence did the work.

James was trapped—caught between fear, loyalty, and control.

By then, I understood that Merly's behavior at the car-cleaning business opening had been only the beginning.

Whenever Devin and I gave James a gift, Merly followed with one of her own. Not thoughtful. Not kind. Flashy. Attention-grabbing. Always designed to overshadow ours.

The timing was deliberate—always after we gave something, always ensuring James knew she was "doing more."

Eventually, Salina delivered the final instruction through James.

"No more gifts."

The words were gentle, but the meaning was sharp: you cannot win here.

It was jealousy, plain and simple.

They couldn't match Devin's care, and they hated that his father could see it.

By 2021, when Devin bought James a coffee machine for Christmas, Salina noticed something she didn't like: Miles and Merly could no longer keep up. Devin's gifts were thoughtful, practical, and meaningful—making Miles and Merly's gifts appear inadequate by comparison.

Salina intervened.

She quietly instructed James to refuse any further gifts from us.

The message, delivered politely, was framed as concern:

"We don't need anything anymore."

But the subtext was clear: stop making them look bad.

What should have been moments of warmth became contests. Every gesture of care was twisted, evaluated, and diminished. Salina ensured that Miles and Merly retained superiority in James's eyes, while Devin's generosity was turned against him.

Then, one Christmas in 2022, she altered the performance.

James must have said something to her—suggested, perhaps, that she give me a gift.

We were seated at the dining table when Salina placed a small box in front of me. She slid it across the polished surface as though fulfilling a requirement rather than offering kindness.

Her lips curved into a practiced smile.

"Go on," she said.

I opened the box.

Inside lay a silver necklace, delicate at first glance, set with an oval blue sapphire. For a brief moment, it looked like something generous. Something thoughtful.

Then I saw the chain.

The clasp was broken.

Not loose. Not worn. Broken cleanly—rendered unusable. A necklace that could not be worn.

While this petty competition played out, something far more serious was unfolding.

In late 2022 and into 2023, James developed a serious wound on his knee that became infected. According to James, he was with Merly when the wound first occurred, and she applied cream to it using her hands. However, the wound worsened.

Merly argued with James's doctor, reprimanding him for not "fixing" it fast enough, while insisting she was doing everything right. James later recounted the confrontation himself.

By April 2023, the infection had spread, and James was hospitalized. His knee was heavily bandaged, and his care was largely controlled by Salina, Miles, and Merly. They restricted information, with medical updates going through them first, keeping Devin at arm's length.

When James finally began speaking freely—though cautiously and hesitantly—I recorded what he told us. The details sent a chill through me.

By August 2023, James's condition had worsened significantly. The wounds were bleeding heavily and had gone untreated for weeks.

On my advice, Devin went to collect his father unannounced.

Salina was caught off guard. She hadn't expected us to take action.

She was on the phone when we arrived, describing James's condition to Miles and Merly. Unable to meet our eyes, she refused to join us at the hospital.

Watching her uneasiness, I remembered one incident before, when we visited James around 2019. He had a black eye on his left eye. When Devin asked him about the bruise on his eye, he gave a strange, awkward laugh. He said he fell on the floor because he was drunk. I watched her do the same thing she always did-pretending to be busy in the kitchen.

He was bandaged all over his body as the infection spread like blisters across his skin. The bleeding persisted for weeks. The cause remained unclear. One doctor speculated it might be a rare condition in elderly patients, often triggered by open wounds that became infected due to poor hygiene or improper care.

Despite being prescribed medication, the bleeding continued.

Only after consulting my overseas relatives in the medical field did his condition begin to improve, following the introduction of high-dose vitamin C. His recovery was slow, but it was finally visible.

By then, the pattern had become unmistakable.

James's vulnerability—his age, illness, and past alcoholism—was being used as leverage.

Gifts.

Medical access.

Information.

Presence.

All controlled to isolate Devin and strip him of influence.

Even the smallest details were manipulated.

In 2023, Devin gave his father a new Telstra mobile phone after his old one broke during a hospital stay. Three weeks later, the phone malfunctioned. The battery was corroded, as if exposed to hot water.

Shortly after, Salina showed us the flip phone Merly had given James as a replacement.

Most of Devin's gifts disappeared from the house, while others were replaced quietly. Everything he offered became invisible. Despite this, Devin continued to believe—for a time—that he could make a difference. He thought love and persistence might still change things.

He believed Salina loved him. He thought Merly was merely difficult, not dangerous. He had no idea how deeply he was being undermined.

By then, it was clear: they weren't just jealous—they were erasing him.

CHAPTER TWELVE

Breaking the Silence

By November 2023, James was beginning to recover from the infected wounds that had once covered much of his body. The bleeding had eased, and the swelling subsided. The vitamin C regimen we had quietly introduced—on the advice of relatives in the medical field—had made a visible difference. For the first time in months, his skin began to heal instead of deteriorating. His appetite returned in small increments. His voice grew steadier. He even laughed once, softly, at something Devin said, as if remembering how to do it.

For a moment, we allowed ourselves to hope.

That hope did not last.

Not long after his condition stabilized, the doctors delivered news that changed everything. James was diagnosed with stomach cancer. The prognosis was cautious, but grim. Without ceremony, we were told he might have as little as a year to live.

The diagnosis didn't bring compassion into the room.

It brought calculation.

From that moment on, Salina and Merly became colder, sharper, and more territorial. Their movements around James shifted. His time was rationed. His visitors filtered. His phone is monitored. Updates on his condition were selectively delivered, often delayed or distorted by the time they reached Devin.

Salina informed us with unsettling bluntness.

"He's dying soon," she said flatly, as if she were announcing a schedule rather than a terminal illness.

There was no tremor in her voice. No sadness. No fear. Only expectation.

I remember watching her eyes as she spoke. They didn't linger on James. They didn't soften. They looked forward, past him, as if his death were already a given—something inevitable, something useful.

It became painfully clear what was unfolding.

They were preparing to take everything:

The house.

The assets.

The authority.

Even his dignity.

And to do that, Devin had to be removed from the equation.

By December 2024—nearly a year after the doctors' timeline—James finally broke his silence.

It happened unexpectedly, during a visit to the house. The atmosphere was tense but deceptively calm. Salina moved about the kitchen with exaggerated busyness, washing dishes that were already clean, rearranging items that didn't need rearranging.

I asked James how he was feeling, about his wounds, and whether he had called for help when he needed it.

He looked at me for a long moment.

Then, suddenly, he pointed.

"Tell her," he said, his finger trembling as it extended toward Salina. "Tell her."

The room stilled.

"When I fell in the bathroom," he continued, his voice low but urgent, "I was stuck. Between the shower doors. I couldn't move."

Salina didn't turn around.

"She didn't call for help," he said. "She didn't call anyone. I was there for hours."

My chest tightened.

"I was calling out," he whispered. "I was scared. I couldn't get up. I thought I was going to die there."

I asked gently, "James... what happened next?"

He swallowed hard.

"She just… left me," he said. "I had to find the strength myself."

When we looked at Salina, she was still at the sink, her back to us, scrubbing the same spot on a plate with unnecessary force. She didn't respond. Didn't acknowledge his words.

In that moment, something inside Devin broke open.

I recorded part of James's confession on video. My hands shook. I was afraid—not just of what he was saying, but of the consequences of documenting it. But fear no longer outweighed necessity.

For the first time, Devin was hearing the truth—without filters.

Not through whispers.

Not through implication.

Not through excuses.

But directly, from his father's mouth.

It didn't stop there.

Over the next hour, James spoke haltingly, cautiously, as though testing whether it was safe to continue. Years of conditioning don't disappear overnight. Even then, his eyes kept flicking toward the kitchen—toward the women who had ruled his life for decades.

"She controls everything," he said at one point. "I don't know what I'm allowed to say anymore."

He told us how medical information had been withheld, how appointments were changed by her order, how doctors spoke to others instead of him, how decisions were made "for his own good" without ever asking him what he wanted.

As he spoke, the puzzle pieces fell into place.

The corroded phone battery.

The replaced gifts.

The sudden absence of Devin from the house.

None of it was random.

It was a strategy.

For years, Devin had believed he was loved—favored, even. He had believed the praise meant protection. But now, he saw it for what it had always been.

Control.

And that realization hollowed him out.

"They used me," he said later, sitting beside me.

"Didn't they?"

I didn't answer immediately. He already knew.

The final fracture came when he realized how deeply Merly and Miles had positioned themselves to inherit James's house. Under the guise of separation, Miles had moved back in. Merly followed soon after. Together, they established themselves as caretakers, decision-makers, and gatekeepers.

Access to James became conditional.

And we were no longer welcome.

That's when Devin made his decision.

Not impulsively.

Not out of anger.

But with a clarity that frightened him.

He would report Merly.

Not for revenge.

But to protect his father—and himself.

It was a terrifying prospect. Devin was illiterate. He struggled with paperwork, statements, and formal processes that required precision. The system itself felt designed to exclude men like him. Yet for the first time in his life, he was choosing confrontation over submission.

"We can't undo the past," he said quietly one night. "But we're not letting them control the future. Not anymore."

The decision alone felt like crossing a line he had been trained never to approach. Fear pressed against him from every side—fear of retaliation, disbelief, and dismissal.

But something fundamental had shifted.

The silence had broken.

What came next remained uncertain—the police response, the weight of the evidence, the truth surfacing after so many years buried beneath obedience and fear. But for the first time, the path forward—however dangerous—belonged to him.

The house. The inheritance. The years of manipulation. They could not all be undone.

But the truth had finally been spoken. Once spoken, it could not be taken back.

CHAPTER THIRTEEN

The Wall of Silence

I reported the incident anonymously. Not because I was unsure of what had happened, but because I already understood the machinery I was up against. Decades of manipulation don't unravel simply because the truth is spoken aloud. They cling, resist, and protect themselves through fear, loyalty, and silence.

When the police first reached out, they contacted Devin.

And that's when the wall rose again.

Years of conditioning flooded him all at once. Every lesson he'd been taught since childhood resurfaced instinctively: family first, don't shame your mother, keep problems inside the home. He still loved her—or at least, the version of her he had been trained to believe in. He still wanted to think there was something redeemable left, some explanation that made her actions less unforgivable.

So, when the police asked him to confirm what had happened—the fall, the hours his father was left trapped, the refusal to call for help—Devin froze. Without realizing it, he began to soften the truth.

"Yes, it happened," he said carefully. "But... my mum didn't mean it like that. She was overwhelmed."

He didn't lie outright. He minimized. He redirected. He protected.

It was reflex. Not intention. A survival mechanism honed over a lifetime.

I had already handed over the recordings, the timeline, and the documented pattern of neglect and control. James's own words described how he had fallen in the bathroom, wedged between the shower doors, calling out for help that never came. The hours he spent trapped on the floor—afraid, in pain, unable to move.

For a moment, it felt like justice might finally be within reach.

But then, the old patterns reasserted themselves.

The police contacted James next. He told us afterward that they had asked him directly about the fall, about the neglect, about whether help had been refused.

James hesitated.

And then—just like Devin—he covered for her.

"She's my wife," he said. "We've been married for over forty years."

He spoke as though longevity excused everything, as if decades of control, silence, and emotional erosion were just the wear and tear of marriage, time absolving harm.

That was enough.

The police closed the case.

Despite recordings.

Despite timelines.

Despite a confession spoken in fear and pain.

Loyalty and conditioning did what outright denial never could:

They erased accountability, but not the truth.

After that, I documented everything—the police calls, the conversations, the visible struggle Devin endured as he realized what he had just done. Not because I wanted to weaponize it, but because I needed proof of something deeper: the long-term psychological control that had shaped both men's responses.

That control was the true crime.

The night Devin decided to formally report Merly's actions online felt different.

Not triumphant.

Heavy.

He sat quietly for a long time before opening the laptop. His shoulders were tense, his jaw set. He read each question slowly, carefully, asking me to repeat words, explain phrasing, and help him navigate the language of authority that had always intimidated him.

But this time, he didn't back away.

"I can't keep letting her get away with it," he said, his voice steady despite the fear underneath. "If I don't protect Dad, no one will."

For the first time, I saw him not shrinking—but bracing.

We prepared everything together. I helped him describe the pattern of manipulation, the interference in family relationships, and the control his father's interactions had been under. We attached dates, context, and corroborating details. It was meticulous—careful, grounded in fact, not emotion.

And yet, even as Devin tried to do the right thing, the damage of decades lingered.

His hands shook.

He second-guessed himself.

He worried about retaliation—about disbelief, being blamed.

"It's not your fault," I told him softly. "This is what they've done to you your whole life. They trained you to protect them, to silence yourself, to forget yourself."

He nodded, but the weight didn't lift.

Even in that moment of courage, he was still bound by the very chains he was trying to break.

And James—who had finally begun to speak—was still, at his core, Salina's prisoner.

I don't think James ever fully believed he was allowed to be angry, or hurt, or betrayed. He had spent too long being taught that survival meant compliance and that peace meant silence. Even when he spoke the truth, he did so with one eye always turned toward his wife, waiting for correction, punishment, or withdrawal.

That is what decades of control do.

They don't just silence you.

They make you doubt your right to speak at all.

And yet—something had shifted.

The wall of silence had cracked. Not fallen. Not yet. But cracked.

Devin had tried. He had taken the first step—imperfect as it was—toward confronting a system designed to keep him small and obedient.

He could see the pattern clearly now: the way loyalty was used as a leash, the way love was confused with protection, the way silence was praised as virtue.

For the first time, the words sounded real.

Not just to me, but to him.

The wall still stood—thick, reinforced by years of fear and manipulation—but it was no longer seamless.

Once a wall cracks, it can never pretend to be solid again.

CHAPTER FOURTEEN

Taking a Stand

In the end, Devin made the decision himself. It wasn't sudden, and it wasn't dramatic. It came after years of being pushed aside, spoken over, quietly erased. After watching his father weaken under control disguised as care. After seeing his own efforts—his concern, his presence, his attempts to help—systematically undermined.

He decided to lodge a formal complaint against Merly.

Not out of anger, and not out of revenge, but because silence had become more dangerous than speaking.

The complaint outlined years of interference: repeated obstruction of contact with his father, involvement in medical decisions without transparency, manipulation of family dynamics, and sustained efforts to position herself as the central authority in James's life. It was written carefully and factually, grounded in what could be demonstrated rather than what was merely felt.

I provided what I had kept for years—recordings, timelines, notes. Not interpretations, but documentation. Evidence of gifts disappearing and being replaced. Evidence of medical information being filtered or withheld. Evidence of how James's access to his own son had been restricted and controlled.

For the first time, Devin was not being spoken about.

He was speaking for himself.

"It won't fix everything," he said quietly to me one night after submitting the report. "But it's a start. For the first time, it feels like it's mine."

That moment mattered more than the outcome.

Because choosing to act—after a lifetime of being conditioned not to—was itself a victory.

It was also then, after long discussion and hesitation, that Devin agreed this story should be written.

Not as an act of accusation, but as a record.

He understood what it meant to place his life on the page—to name patterns he had once been taught to excuse, to allow his experiences to stand without apology, and to tell the truth while it was still intact. He wanted what had happened to be documented before it could be softened, rewritten, or buried again by silence. This Book exists with his knowledge and consent, shaped through conversations about what could be shared, what should remain private, and why telling the story mattered.

The years of manipulation had left their mark. On Devin. On James. On me. Relationships were strained. Trust had been eroded. Small kindnesses were treated with suspicion. Even care itself became something to be negotiated, monitored, or undermined.

Gifts disappeared.

Words were twisted.

Medical decisions were redirected.

Silence was rewarded.

And yet, beneath all of it, something endured.

Not rage—but clarity.

Merly's behavior had never been hidden—only reframed. Her involvement was described as a concern. Her interference was helpful. Salina's quiet support ensured that the version of events was held. James, worn down by years of deference, followed the path of least resistance. Miles remained close enough to benefit, distant enough to deny responsibility.

It was a system that relied on silence to survive.

And now, that silence had been broken.

The timelines Devin submitted weren't just evidence; they were protection. A diary of events that could no longer be rewritten. A safeguard against the familiar pattern of denial and minimization.

More importantly, they marked a shift.

Devin wasn't just reporting conduct.

He was reclaiming his voice.

For the first time, he understood that loyalty does not require self-erasure. That protecting the family does not mean protecting harm. That silence, when imposed, is not virtue—it is control.

Whatever followed—whether investigation, resistance, or disappointment—he was no longer navigating blindly. He had stepped into the light with the truth in his hands.

The future remained uncertain. But it was no longer predetermined.

This was not the end of the story.

But it was the end of submission.

And the beginning of something Devin had never truly been allowed before:

Choice.

Author's Note

This book was written with the full knowledge and consent of the person at the center of this story.

It is not an act of revenge, not an attempt to rewrite history, but an effort to document what coercive control can look like when it hides behind family, care, and authority.

Some details have been changed to protect privacy. What has not been changed is the emotional truth of what it is like to grow up believing love and control are the same thing.

This story is shared in the hope that others who recognize parts of themselves in these pages will understand that confusion is not weakness, silence is not loyalty, and clarity is not betrayal.

J.A. Marlowe

www.ingramcontent.com/pod-product-compliance
Lightning Source LLC
Chambersburg PA
CBHW051258020426
42333CB00026B/3262